I Use Simple Machines

by Buffy Silverman

Science Content Editor:
Kristi Lew

Educational Media

rourkeeducationalmedia.com

Science content editor: Kristi Lew

A former high school teacher with a background in biochemistry and more than 10 years of experience in cytogenetic laboratories, Kristi Lew specializes in taking complex scientific information and making it fun and interesting for scientists and non-scientists alike. She is the author of more than 20 science books for children and teachers.

www.rourkeeducationalmedia.com

Photo credits: Cover © kontur-vid, Cover logo frog © Eric Pohl, test tube © Sergey Lazarev;; Page 3 and 22 © ER_09; Page 5 © hamurishi; Page 7 illustrations by Christian Lopetz, © Blue Door Publishing, FL; Page 9 and 22 © Christina Richards; Page 11 and 23 © tr3gin; Page 13 and 23 © Sergey Lavrentev; Page 15; DenisNata © 22 © Blue Door Publishing, FL; Page 17 © Stephen Gibson; Page 19, 23 illustration by Alyssia Sheikh, © Blue Door Publishing, FL; Page 20 © Anatoliy Samara

Editor: Kelli Hicks

Cover and page design by Nicola Stratford, bdpublishing.com

Library of Congress Cataloging-in-Publication Data

Silverman, Buffy.
I use simple machines / Buffy Silverman.
    p. cm. -- (My science library)
Includes bibliographical references and index.
ISBN 978-1-61741-728-3 (Hard cover) (alk. paper)
ISBN 978-1-61741-930-0 (Soft cover)
1. Simple machines--Juvenile literature. I. Title.
TJ147.S549 2010
621.8--dc22
                              2011003760

Rourke Educational Media
Printed in the United States of America,
North Mankato, Minnesota

rourkeeducationalmedia.com

customerservice@rourkeeducationalmedia.com • PO Box 643328 Vero Beach, Florida 32964

Machines are everywhere!
Machines make work easier.

Some machines have many parts. Others have few parts.

A bicycle is a machine with many parts.

Simple machines have few or no moving parts.

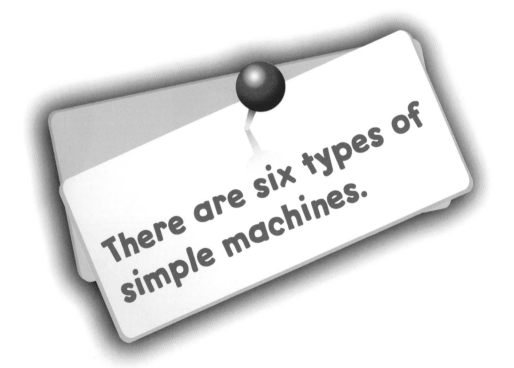

There are six types of simple machines.

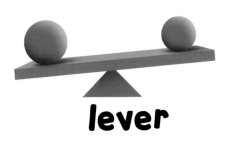

lever

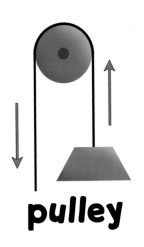

pulley

ramp

screw

wedge

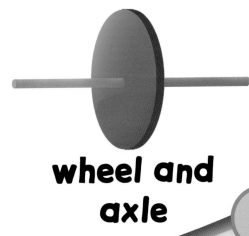

**wheel and
axle**

7

How will he lift this heavy load? He pulls it up a **ramp**.

A ramp is a simple machine for lifting.

9

Some machines cut. A **wedge** splits wood.

An axe is a simple machine that cuts.

11

A **screw** turns. It cuts into wood. It holds things together.

A screw is a simple machine that cuts and holds.

13

Can you lift your friend?
You can with a **lever**!

A seesaw is a simple machine for lifting.

15

Wheels roll. Skateboards ride on wheels. What else has wheels?

axle

wheel

A wheel and axle is a simple machine for moving.

The piano must go up.
A **pulley** helps lift it.

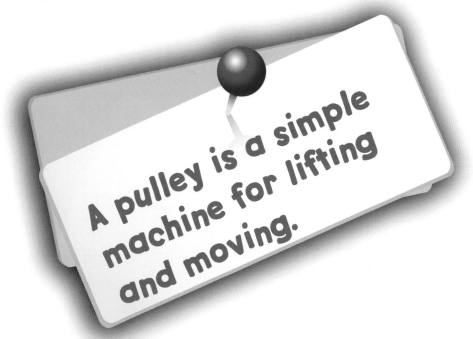

A pulley is a simple machine for lifting and moving.

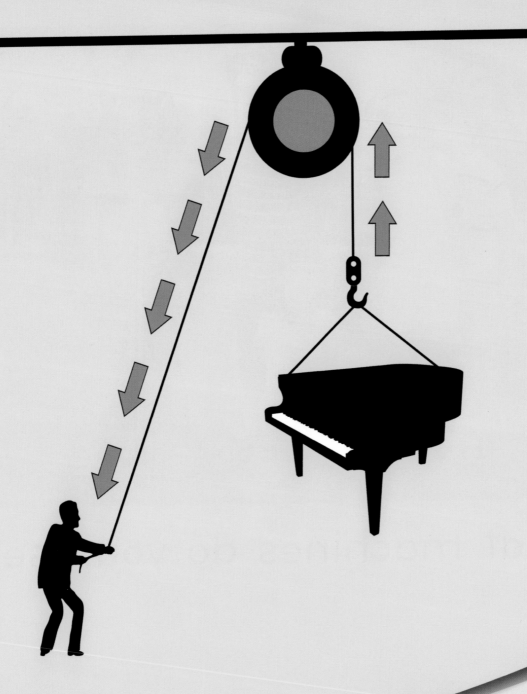

What machines do you use?

1. How do machines help people?

2. What happens to a log when a wedge is pushed into it?

3. Can you name two machines that are used for lifting?

21

Picture Glossary

lever (LEV-ur):
A lever is a bar used to lift or move an object.

machines (muh-SHEENZ):
Machines make it easier to lift, move, cut, or do other work.

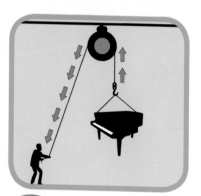

pulley (PUL-lee):
A pulley is a wheel with a groove that a rope runs over. It is used to lift objects.

ramp (RAMP):
A ramp is a sloped surface. Objects are pushed up and down a ramp.

screw (SKROO):
A screw is a fastener that looks like a nail, with threads that spiral around it.

wedge (WEJ):
A wedge is shaped like a V and is used to split objects apart.

Index

Websites

www.edheads.org/activities/simple-machines/

www.mikids.com/Smachines.htm

www.msichicago.org/fileadmin/Activities/Games/
simple_machines/index.php

About the Author

Buffy Silverman loves to watch animals and find wildflowers. She writes about nature and science from her home in Michigan.